MY BODY PARTS

sophie zee

Copyright © 2024 by Sophie Zee.
All rights reserved.

No part of this book may be used or reproduced in any form without prior written permission from the author, except as permitted by U.S. copyright law.

TIPS FOR READING THIS BOOK

When reading this book, try using multi-sensory strategies. Here's an example with the body part "cheeks":
- Say "cheeks" out loud
- Tap the visual of checks on the page
- Tap your own cheeks and say "cheeks"
- Tap your child's cheeks and say "cheeks"

Children learn through repetition & exposure. As adults, that can sometimes feel boring to us, but it's great for kids . It's great for their learning and they enjoy knowing what to expect. Even if your child can't point to body parts yet, it's great to expose them to these concepts and vocabulary!

Make sure to use body part words often outside of reading this book too. For example, when brushing your teeth or your child's say "teeth" or "brushing teeth." You want to use the words often and consistently!

Lets find our...

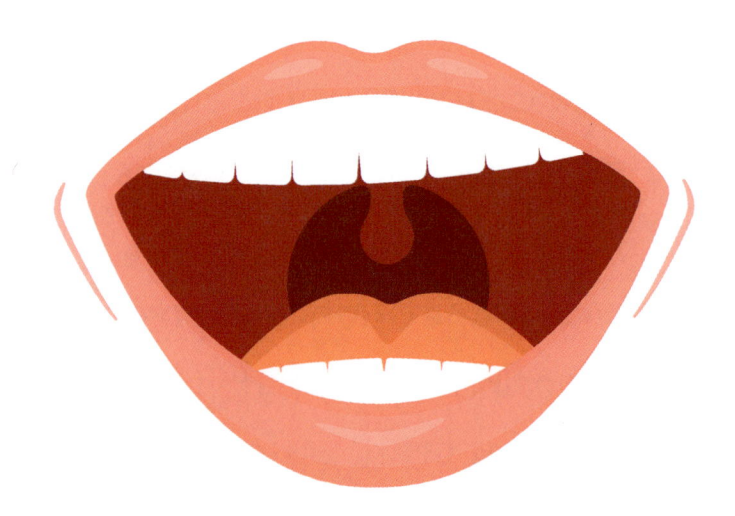

MOUTH

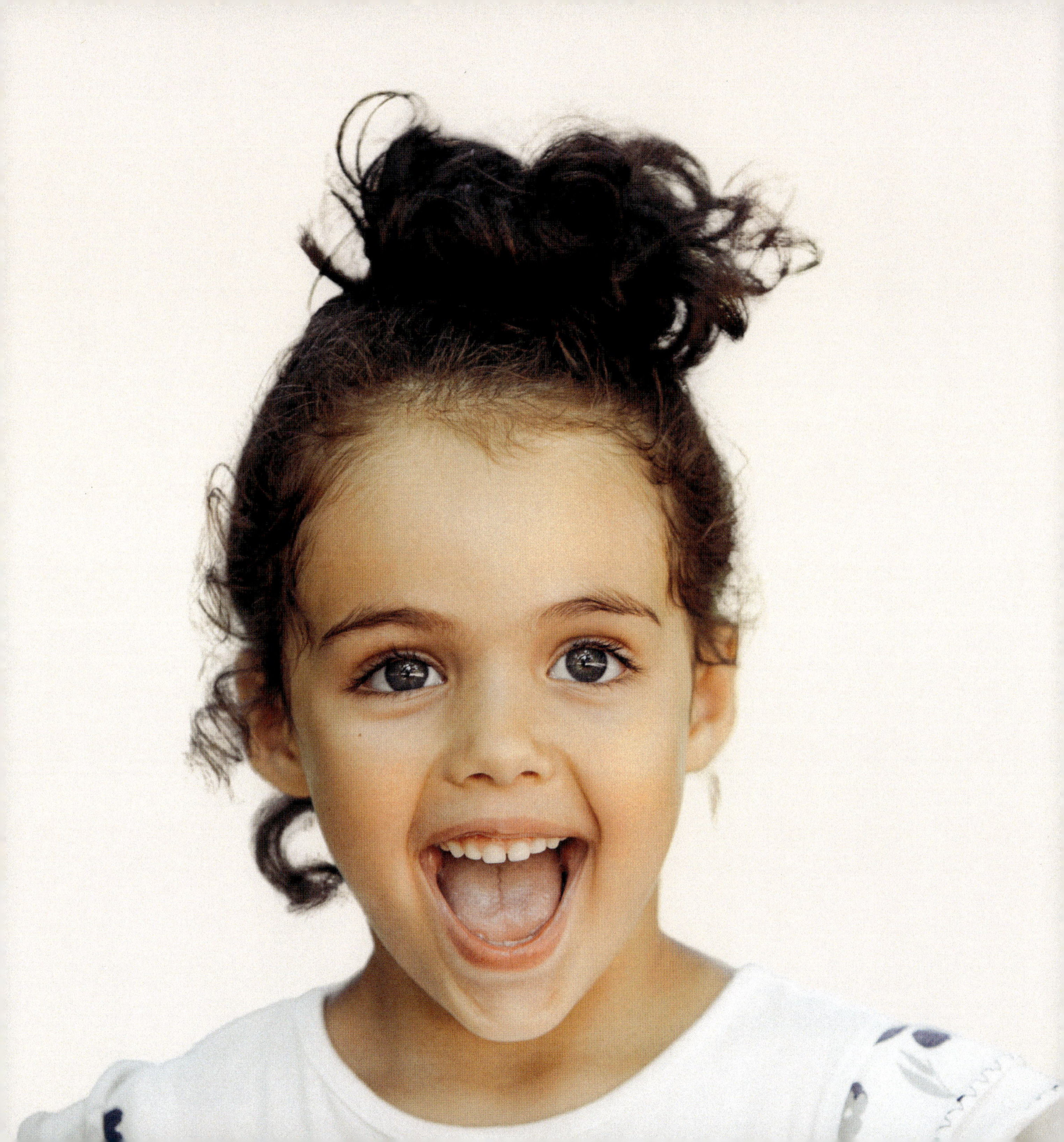

Lets find our...

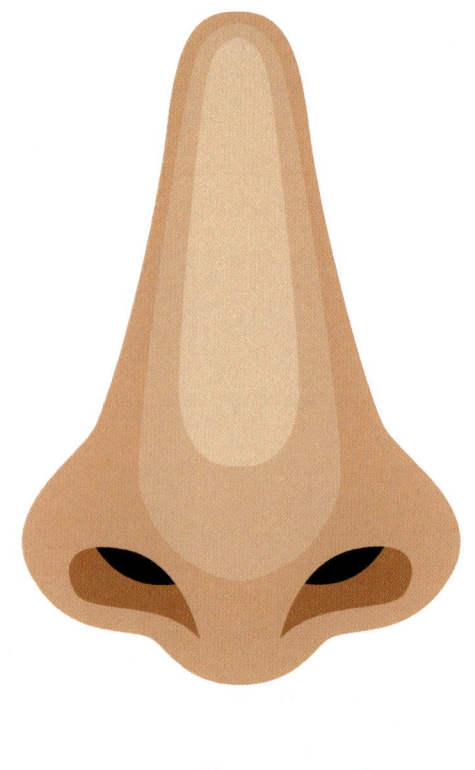

NOSE

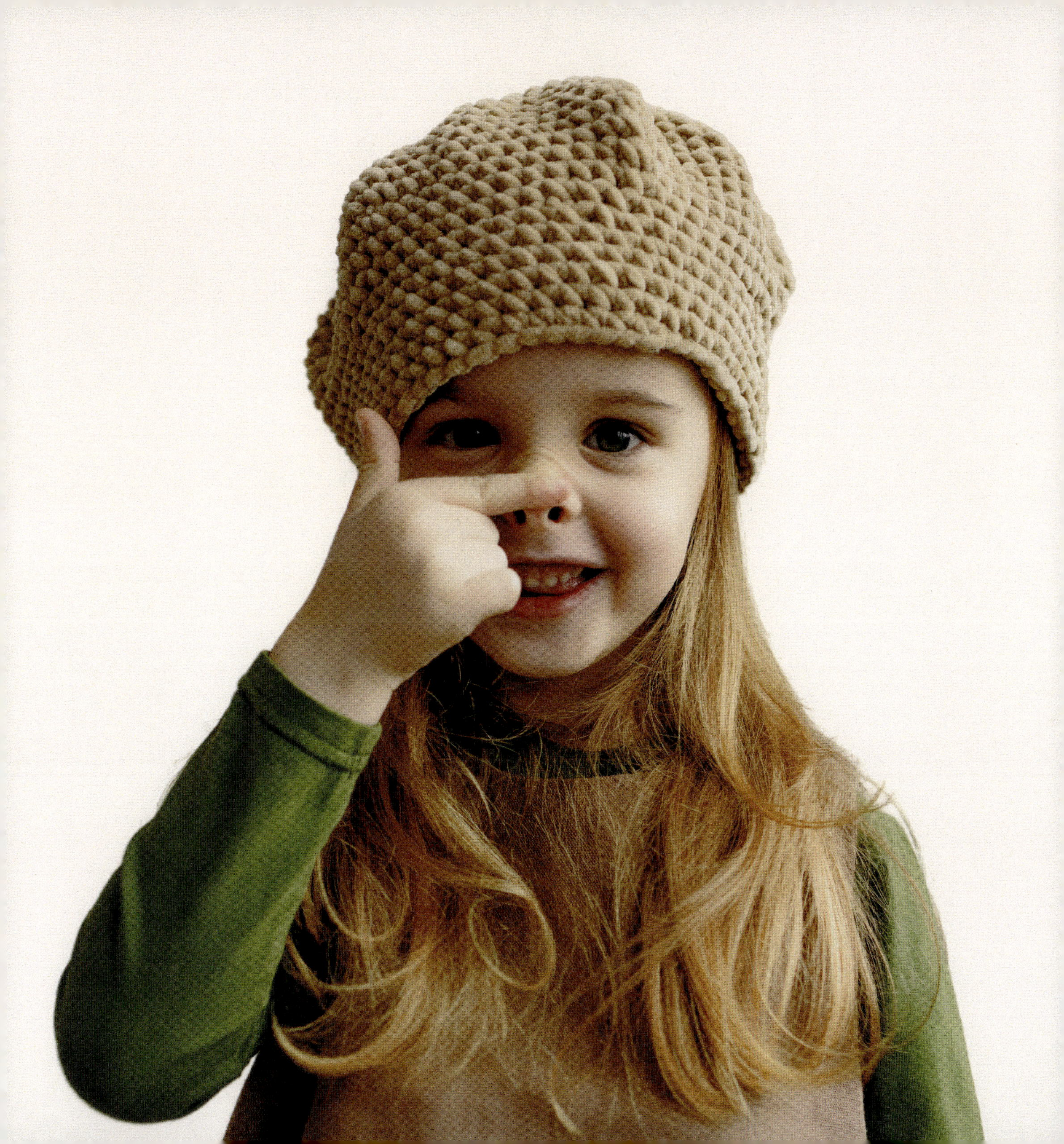

Lets find our...

EYES

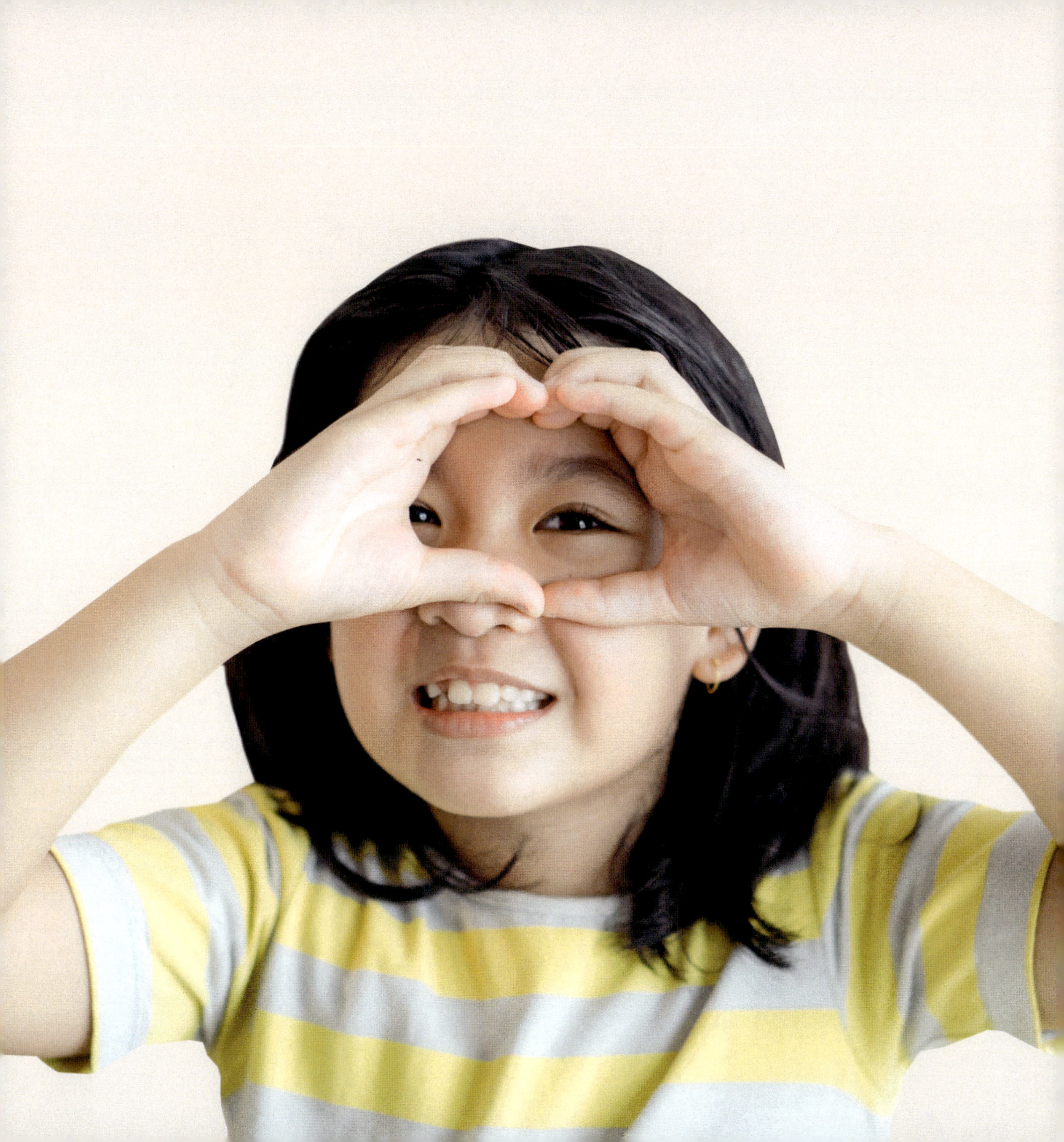

Lets find our...

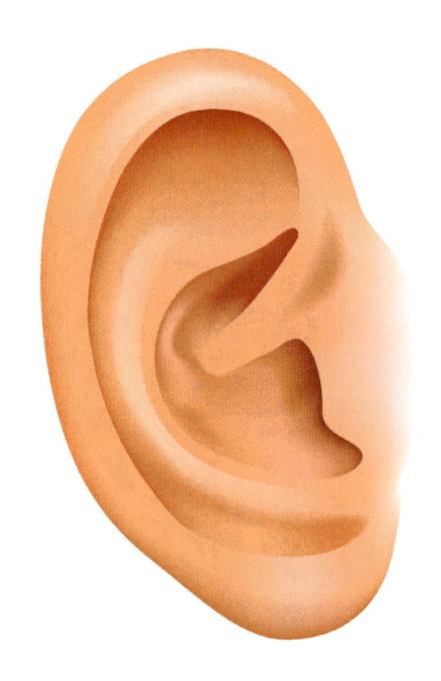

EARS

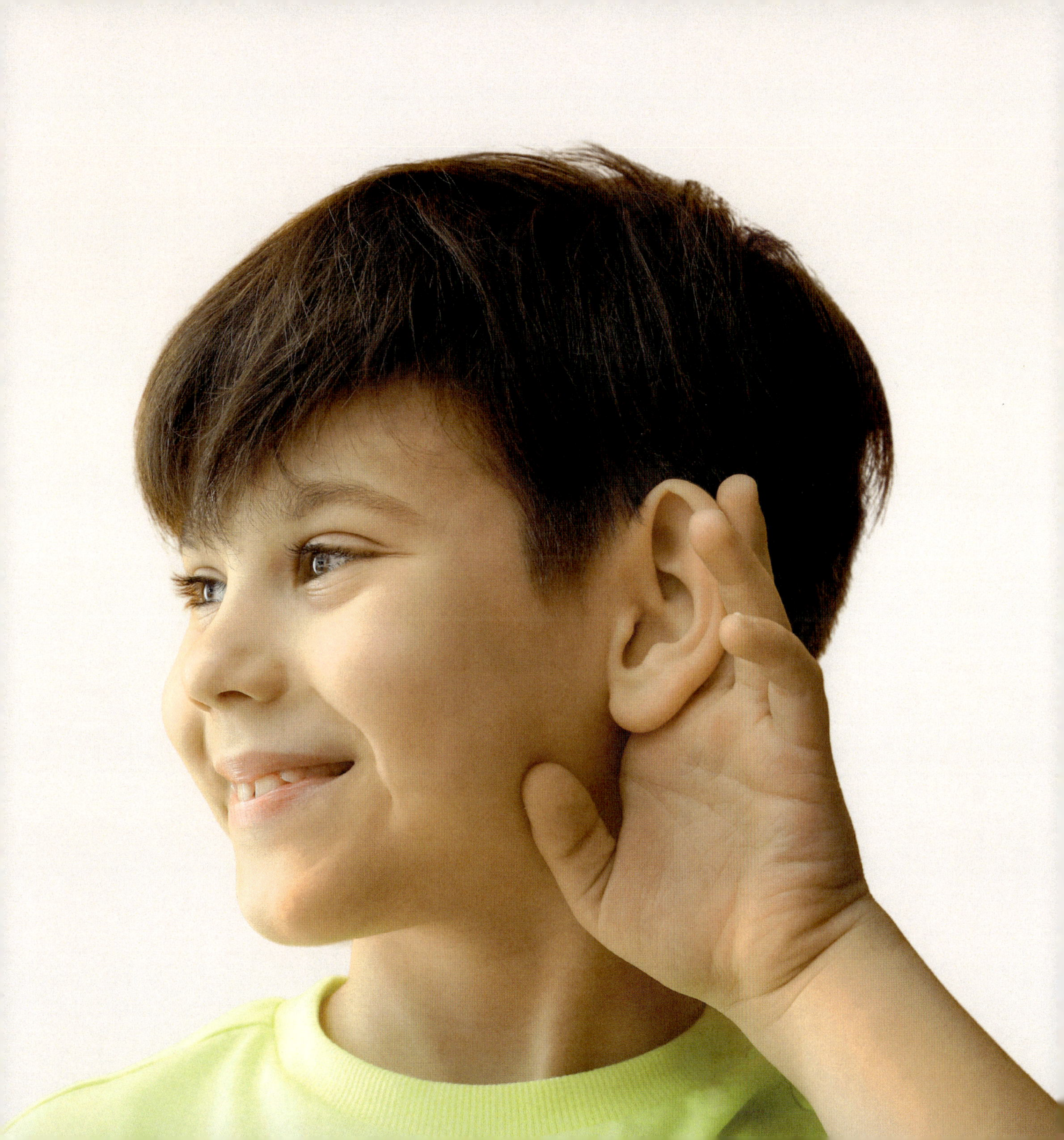

Lets find our...

CHEEKS

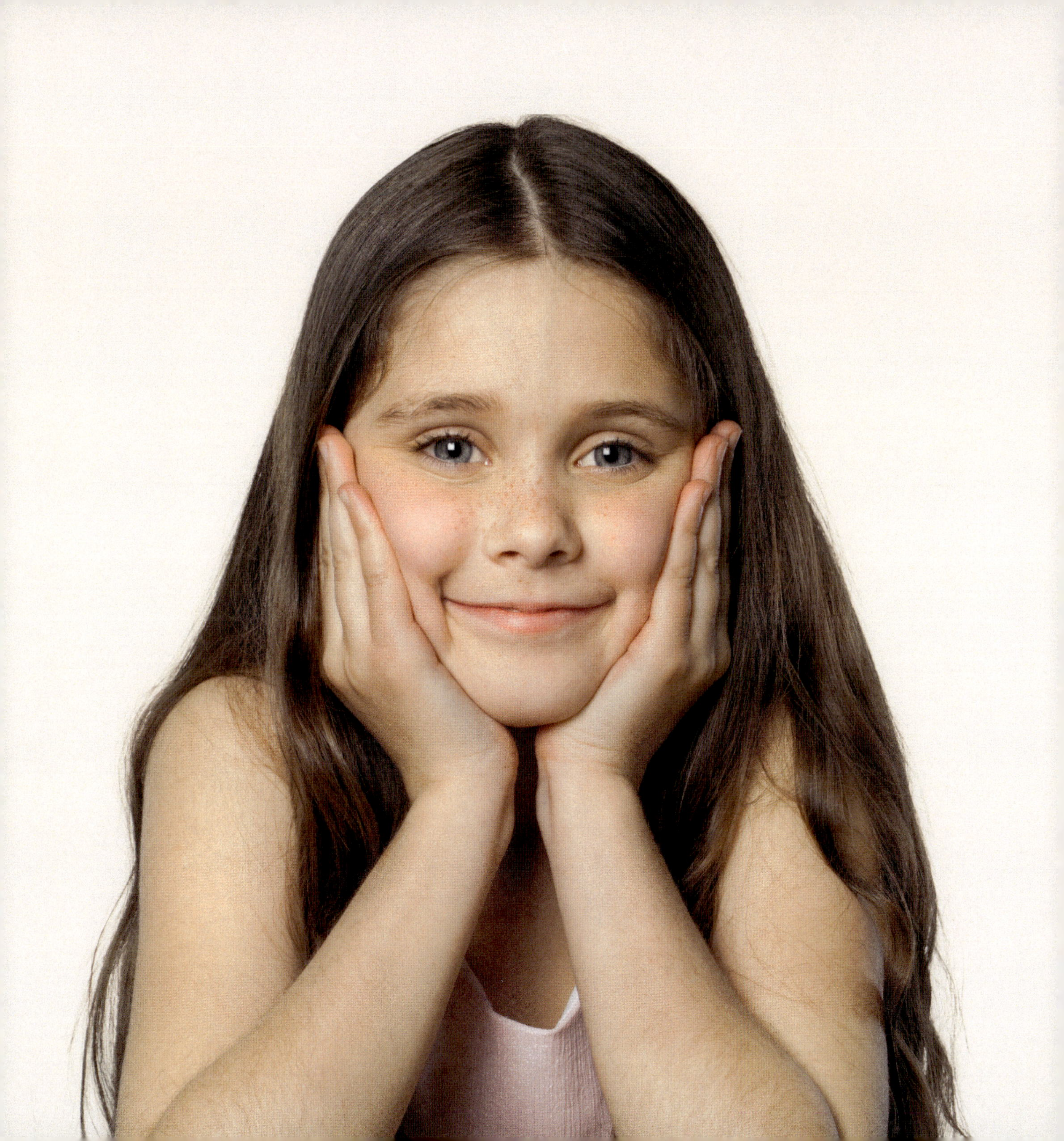

Lets find our...

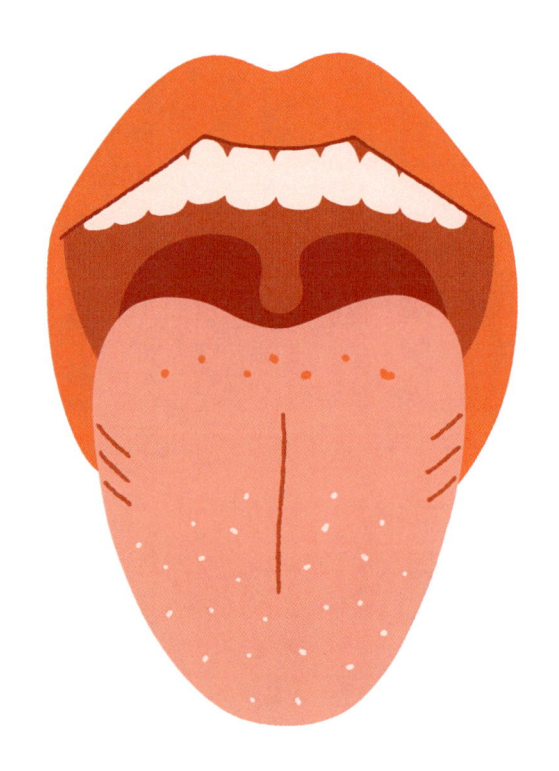

TONGUE

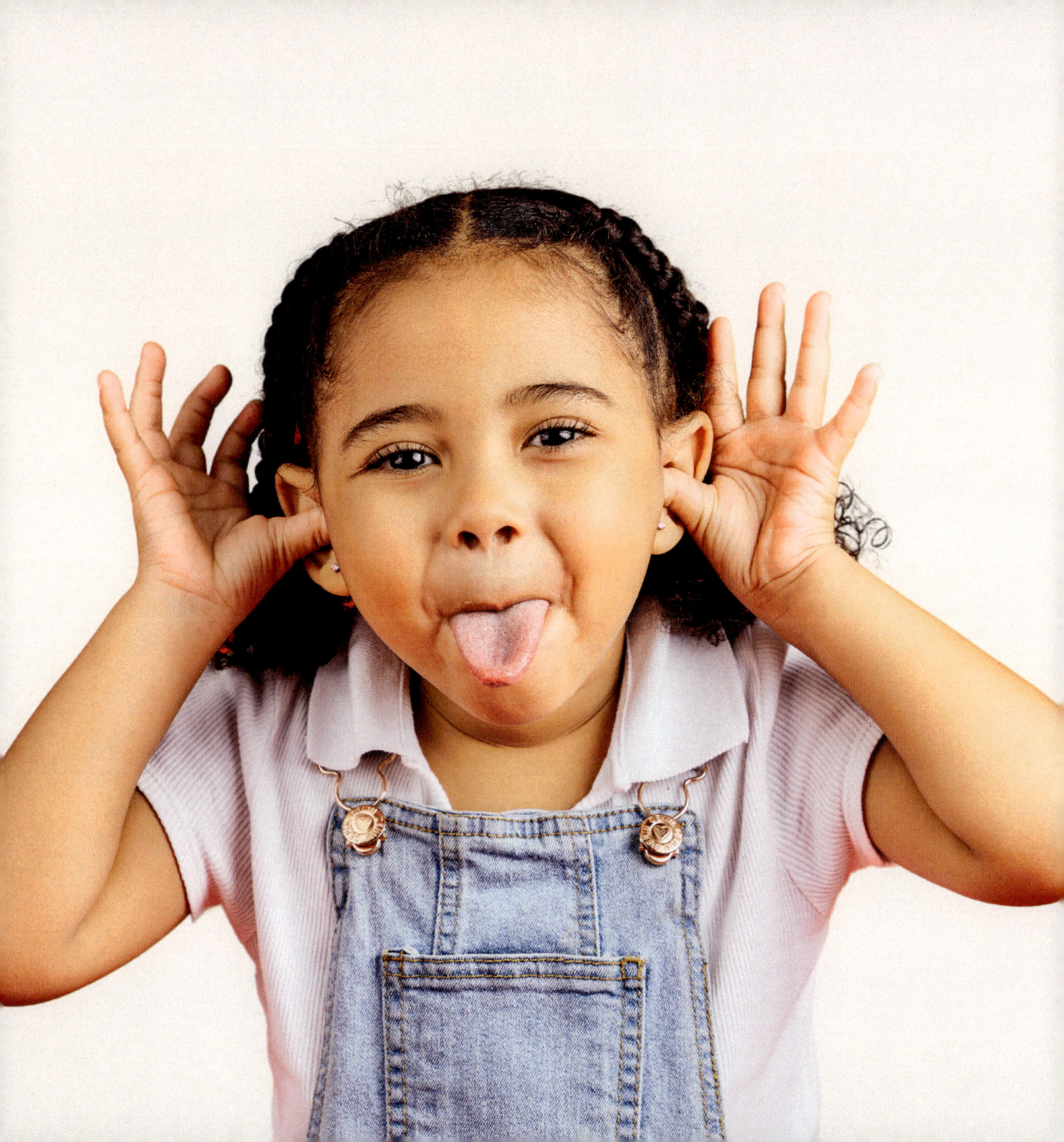

Lets find our...

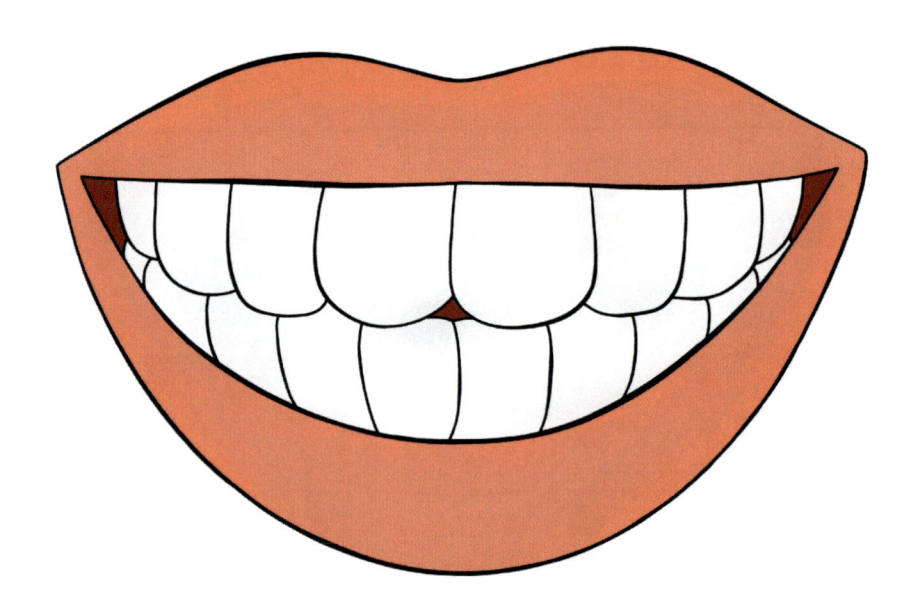

TEETH

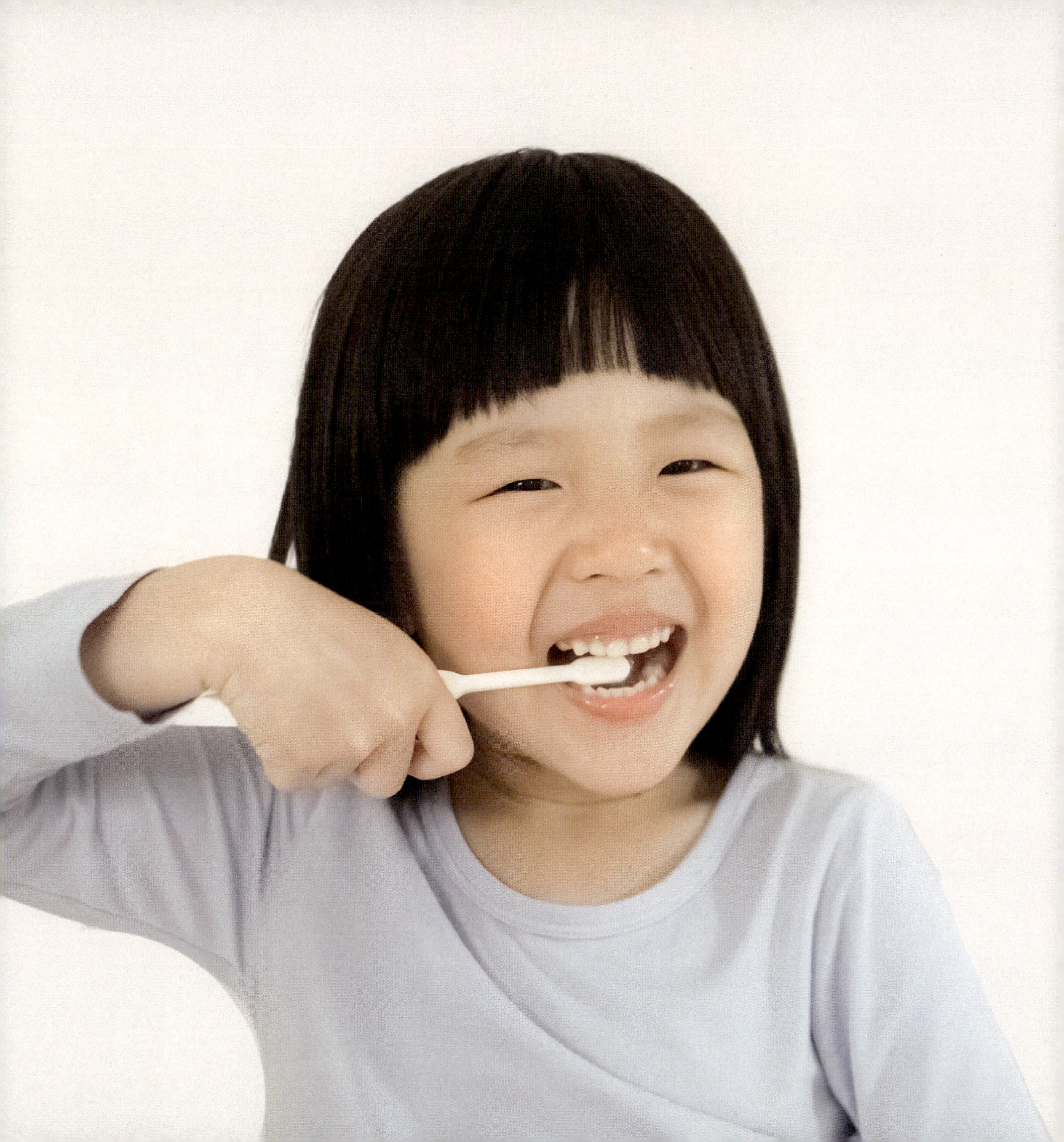

Lets find our...

HEAD

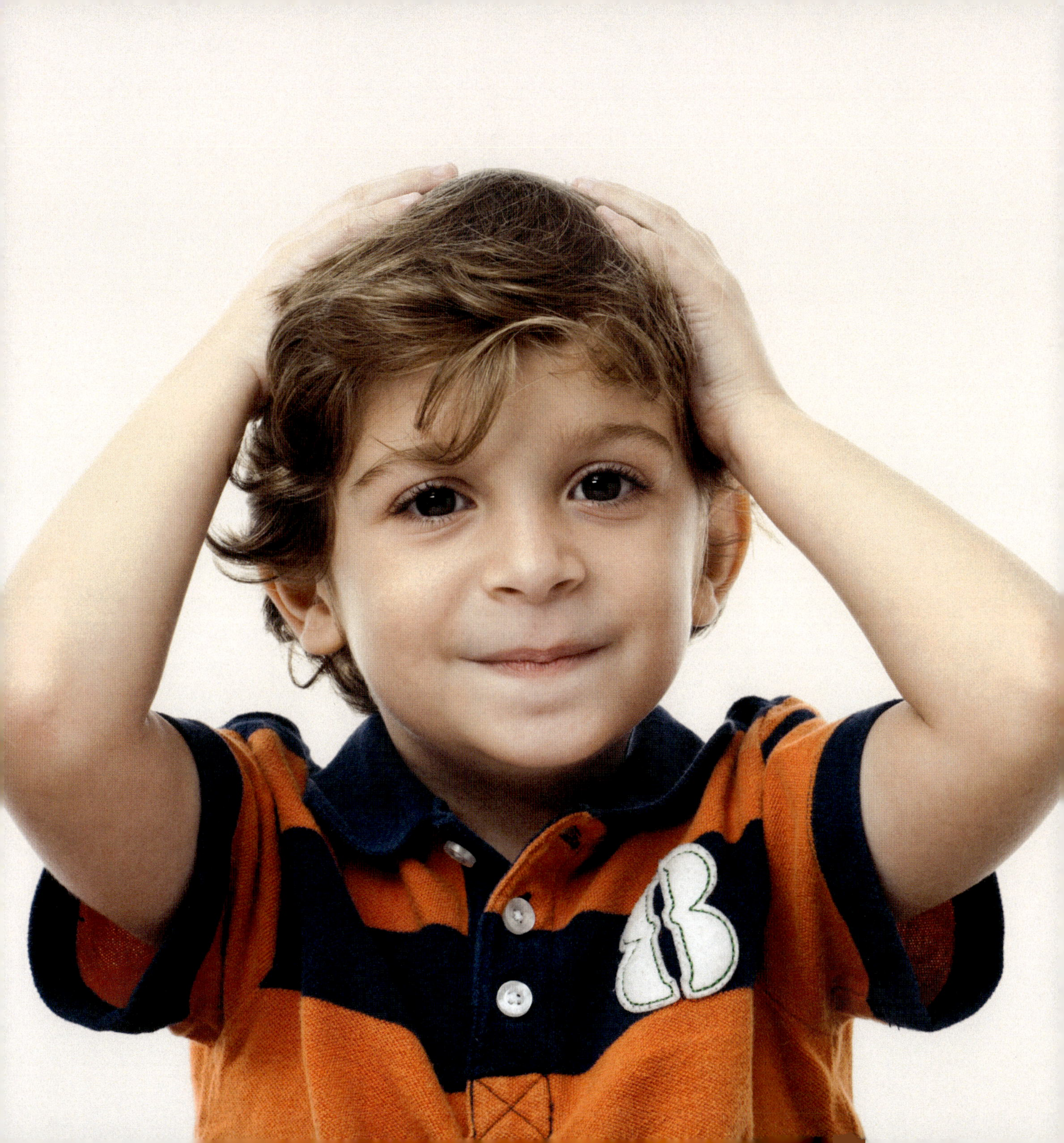

Lets find our...

HANDS

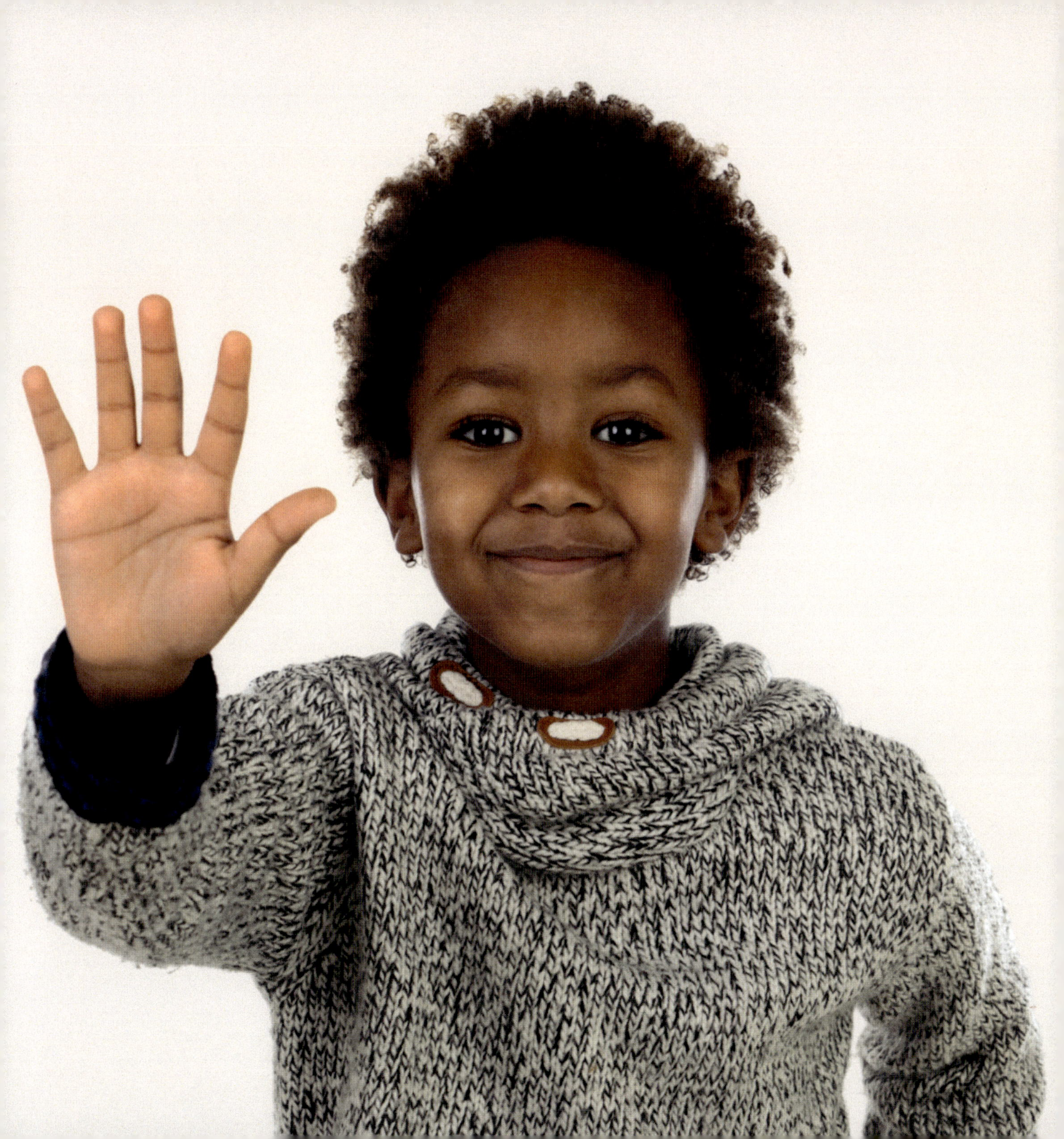

Lets find our...

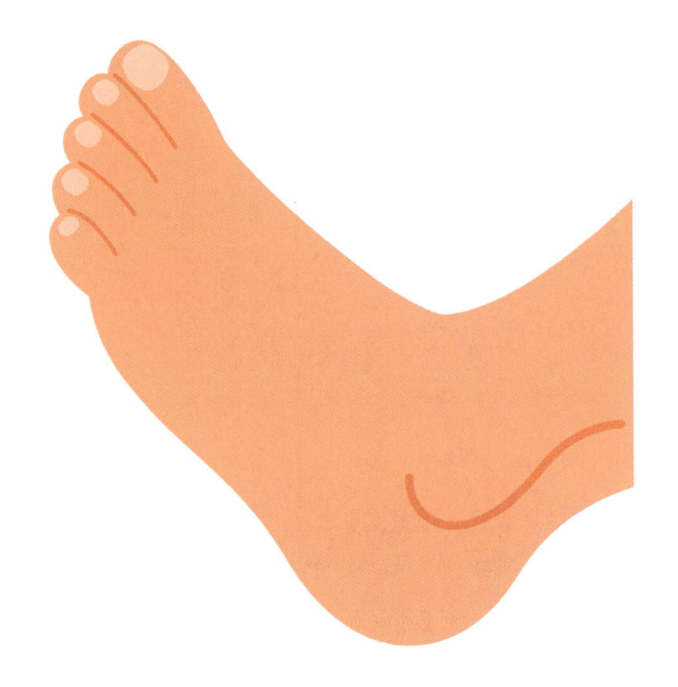

FEET

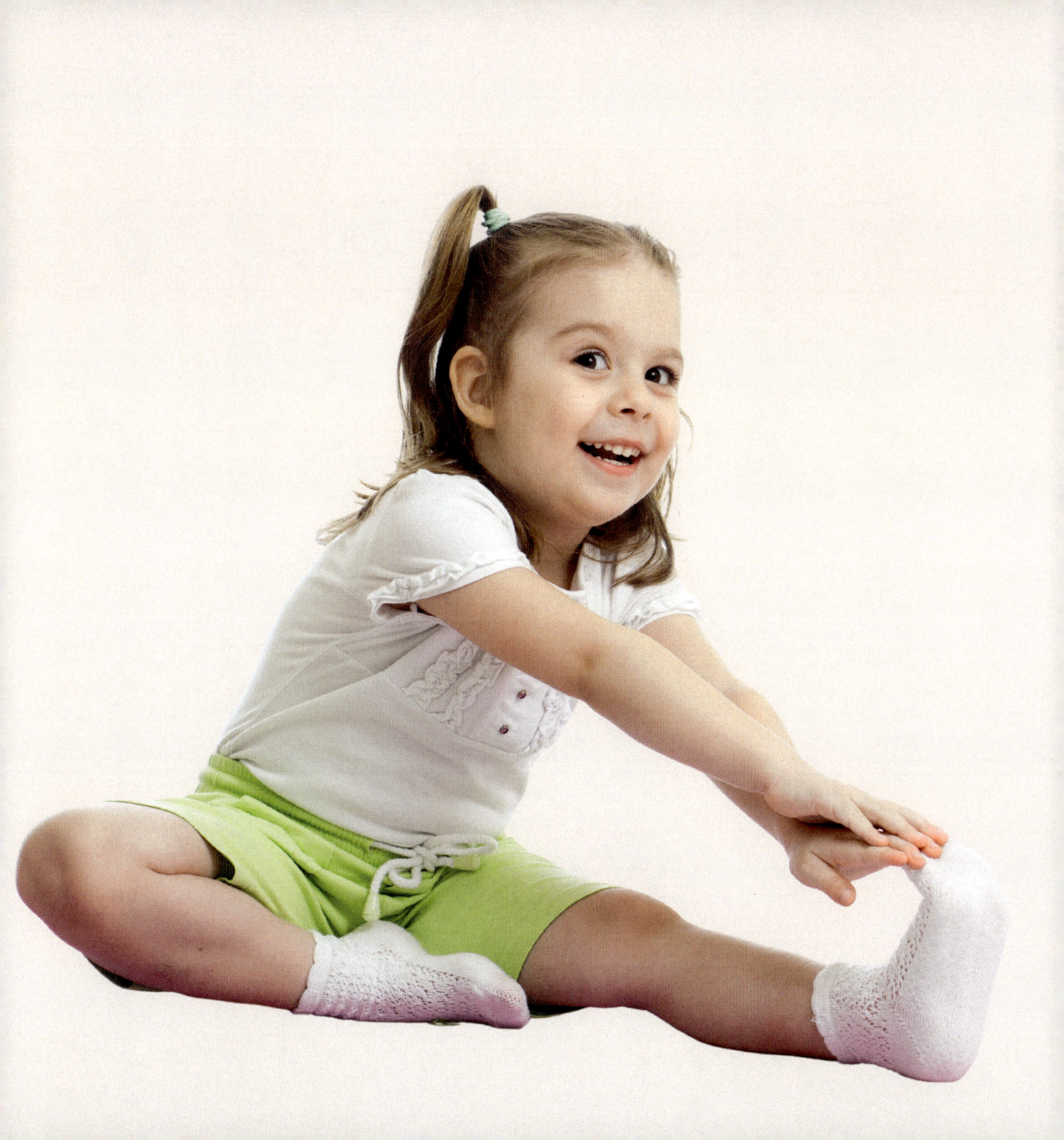

Lets find our...

TUMMY

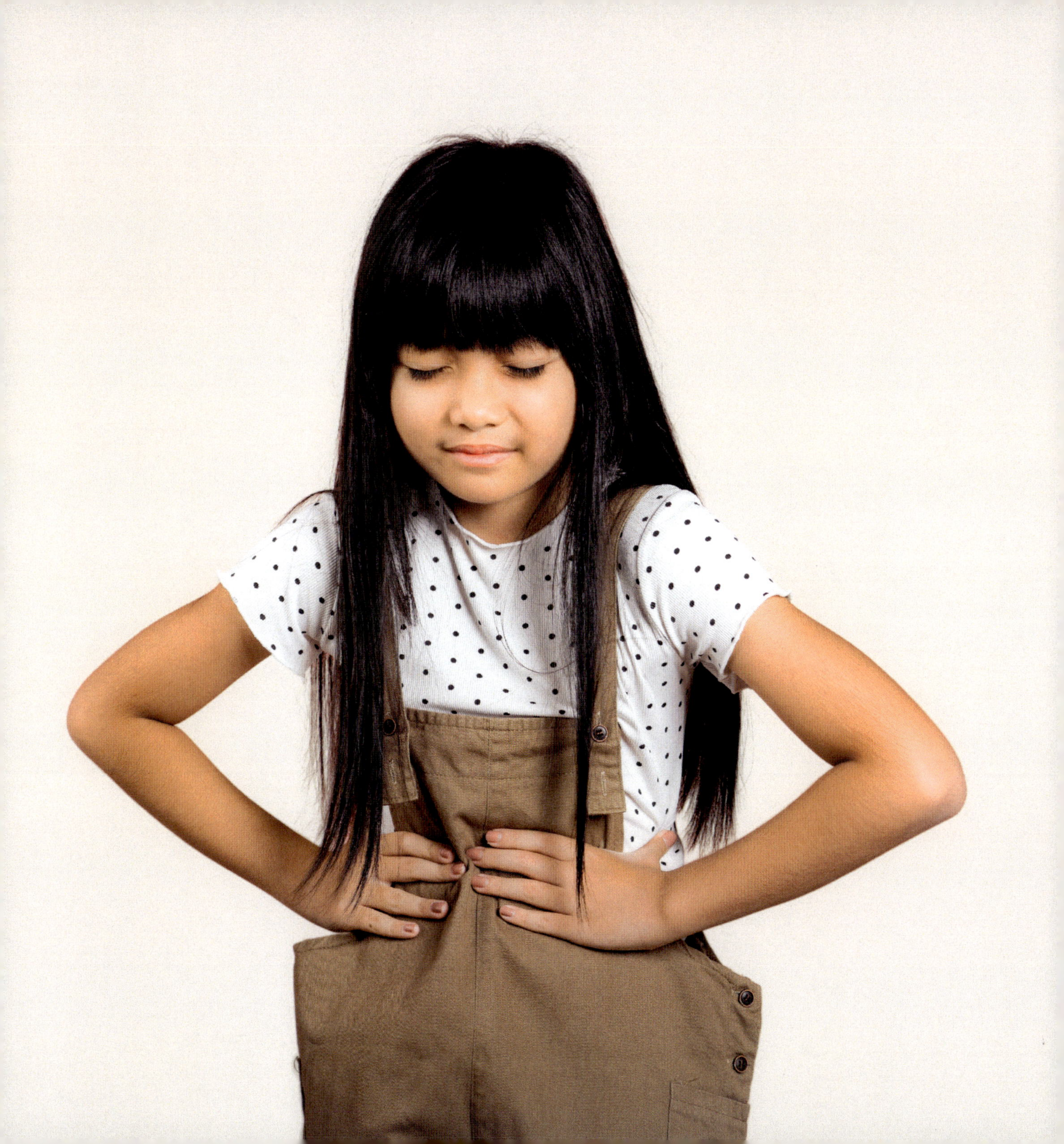

Made in the USA
Coppell, TX
25 March 2025